S0-AIQ-185

0 00 30 0367483 9

How to Cross a Pond

poems about water

by **Marilyn Singer**

illustrated by **Meilo So**

Alfred A. Knopf
New York

In Memory of My Good Friend Easy,
Who Loved to Cross a Pond

Many thanks to Steve Aronson, David Lubar,
Dian Curtis Regan, my wonderful editor Janet Schulman,
and the gang at Random House.

THIS IS A BORZOI BOOK PUBLISHED BY ALFRED A. KNOPF

Text copyright © 2003 by Marilyn Singer
Illustrations copyright © 2003 by Meilo So

www.randomhouse.com/kids

Library of Congress Cataloging-in-Publication Data
Singer, Marilyn
How to cross a pond : poems about water / by Marilyn Singer ;
illustrated by Meilo So.—1st ed.
p.   cm.
Summary: Such poems as "Babbling Brook," "Spring in the Garden,"
"Watercolors," "City River," and "Ocean Checklist"
present some of the many facets of water.
ISBN 0-375-82376-X (trade) — ISBN 0-375-92376-4 (lib. bdg.)
1. Water—Juvenile poetry. 2. Children's poetry, American.
[1. Water—Poetry. 2. American poetry.] I. So, Meilo, ill. II. Title.
PS3569.I546 H69 2003
811'.54—dc21   2002034210

Printed in the United States of America

August 2003

10   9   8   7   6   5   4   3   2   1

First Edition

Contents

Water Music	4
Babbling Brook	6
Dress-Up	8
How to Cross a Pond	10
Lost and Found	12
Spring in the Garden	14
Fair-Weather Friend	16
Watercolors	18
Rain Forest	20
Underwater Ballet	22
Oasis	24
Frog Prince	26
Water Guns	28
City River	30
Wells	32
The Moon's Gravity	34
What Water Can Be	36
Meandering	38
Ocean Checklist	40

Water Music

Water has such a powerful voice
It speaks to ducks and bears and seals
    To salamanders, dragonflies
       albatrosses, eels
To waders, swimmers, sailors, skippers
    of rowboats, schooners, liners, clippers
Water hums lullabies of home
    sings ballads of journeys great and small
Even when it whispers
      we hear water's call
    and answer with need, in hope, by choice
       Water has such a powerful voice

4

Babbling Brook

The brook it really babbles

     It murmurs and it mutters

It's lively and it's sleepy

     It's eloquent, it stutters

What's it telling? What's it saying?

     Is it grave or is it playing?

If my ears were only sharper

     If my tongue a bit less bookish

It would be grand to understand

          and speak with it in Brookish

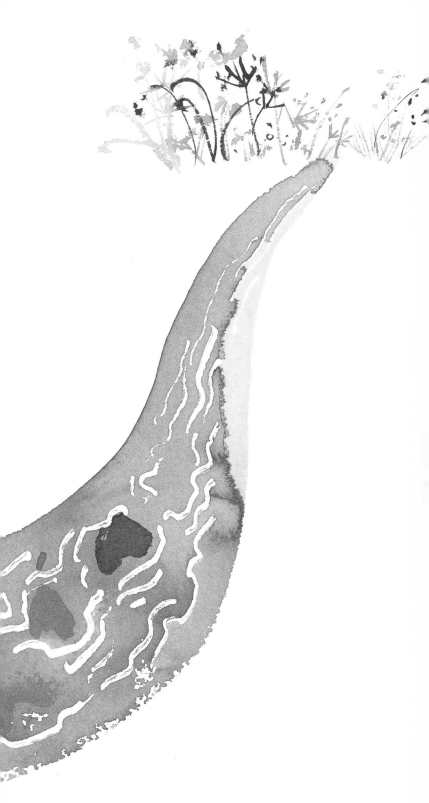

Dress-Up

Each morning in the garden I watch the daily game
of dress-up.
Diamond necklaces of dew or lace collars of frost,
Feathered hats of snow or tiaras of ice.
Water is so excellent a designer—
each fashion unique
and guaranteed to change with every season,
so no tree is ever caught
in yesterday's old clothes.

8

How to Cross a Pond

You can swim
> or you can float
on a raft
> or in a boat.

You can skate
> and you can row.
You can get
> your dog to tow.

You can fly
> if you're a hawk.
And in the winter
> you can walk.

Lost and Found

When the snow melts

    my street becomes a lost-and-found.

There are my mother's earrings, my sister's ball,

    the test I nearly passed, the homework I really lost.

Here are the stoopsitters, hoopshooters, ropejumpers,

    the neighbors I haven't seen since the blizzard came.

Everywhere are the fuzzy buds and tufts of grass,

    the pale shoots and sprouts missing since last March.

When the snow melts

    my street loses its tired, wet winter coat

and finds again its shiny new spring shoes.

Spring in the Garden

In the lotus pool
　　　koi swim; Heron perches
on the No Fishing sign.

In the lotus pool
　　　Duck floats; two drakes argue
about who saw her first.

Fair-Weather Friend

I'm a fair-weather friend to the rain.
A week of it in April and I complain.
No talk of tulips or daisies
        will cancel my crazies.
I've no use for that showers-and-flowers refrain.

But soon, day after midsummer day,
When the sky never seems to turn gray,
I'm so tired of the haze
        and the sun's steady blaze,
I wish the rain would remember to come down
        and play!

Watercolors

Turquoise, teal, aquamarine,
Silver, charcoal, smoke,
          these are the colors of water
we see in sunlight, in rain.
Brown, too, of mud and cattails,
Red of clay,
Yellow of fallen leaves.
And then there's black.
Not the velvet dark at nighttime
          but the deep down fathomless dark
where fish, all teeth and throat,
          drift, glowing by their own light,
or swim sightless in sunless caves far underground.
The black of sleep
          as thorough as only water can allow.
The black we'd have to see
          not to see,
to understand just how black

                              black can be.

18

Rain Forest

In the rain forest, where the ground is a limitless
                    sponge
              drinking in cloud after cloud's worth
                        of water,
the treetops are ablaze with private ponds
          each no bigger than a flower's cup.
Tadpoles hatch within them
          swimming leisurely
          turning into tiny frogs,
                  each one master of its estate
where every petal is a teeming shore
                every pool a boundless lake.

Underwater Ballet

Flower petals
Pumpkinseeds
    Dozing catfish
    Fallen reeds
Tiny feathers
Silver floats
    Dangling goggles
    Little boats
Diving beetles
Dark gray rocks
    Rainbow bubbles
    Drifting socks
Flashing elbows
Sunken logs
    Knobby kneecaps
    Leaping frogs
Trailing fingers
Plumes of spray
    Flapping flippers
      Pond ballet

22

Oasis

If a pond is an oasis
        in the desert
a blessing of palms
        to perching birds
        and travelers grown weary of sand,
Is an island an oasis
        in the ocean?
A gift of palms
        to perching birds
        and travelers grown weary of water
                sailors hungry for a taste of land?

Frog Prince

Down under the wet
                green
my brother dreams
        of a life amphibious.
To swim for hours
        without surfacing,
To breathe through damp
                skin.
In his closet a tangle
        of snorkels, fins,
                goggles and slippery suits
tells the story of so many brave failures:
        No matter how hard he tries
                this prince will never be
                        a frog.

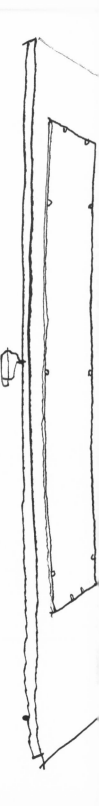

Water Guns

We're having a water war
        A spurt and squirty
          clean but dirty
          I'm-gonna-find-you
          Look-out-behind-you
                        water war
You zap my elbow
        I whap your knee
It's a stalk and a race
        Who will score in the face?
We're all wet
        and we'll get wetter
We've got water on the brain
We're feeling good
        and we'll feel better—
And then it starts
        to rain

City River

Who could believe our sudden summer stream

our splay and spray

just today

waterway

the stubby hydrant brings

is the same wild river that springs

from the melting mountains far away

where hemlocks sway

brook trout stay

otters play

each winter day

Wells

Water is too easy here,
        grandma says.
Taps and toilets,
     hoses and hydrants,
A quick twist, swish, run.
To appreciate water
       you must work for it,
Pump, hoist, and haul.
Learn to love
       the heft of the bucket
         in your hands,
       the weight of the cool jar
         on your head.
Learn to understand
       that water is the true treasure
         of small villages and great cities.
Only then will you never squander
    what is not yours to own.

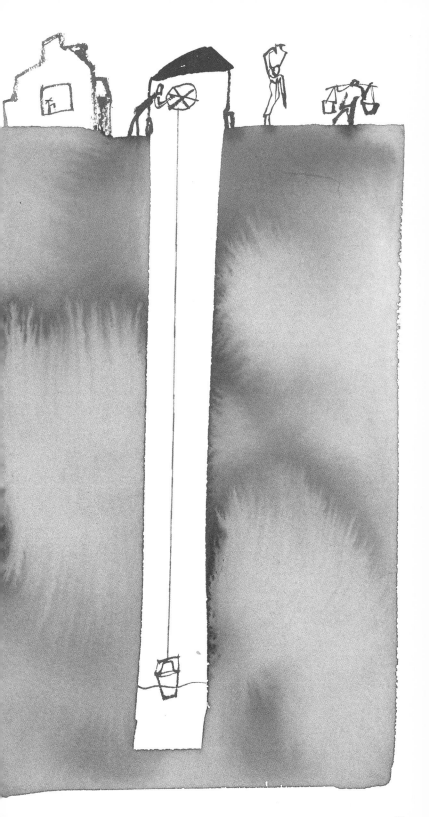

The Moon's Gravity

I feel sorry for the moon
        the dry moon
tugging at the earth's oceans
        as if she could draw them up
                to fill her vast dusty seas
Even Mars
        distant Mars
 it seems has real water
        where tiny creatures may perhaps lie

                                multiply

        under a layer of rock
But the moon
        the poor moon
must make do with memories
        of tall, two-legged visitors
who stopped briefly by years ago
        then returned to their blue planet
to gaze at her tearless face
        and feel her dragging the waves
                from under their sandy feet

What Water Can Be

A furrow that's filling
　　　Water, collective
Your face in the puddle
　　　Water, reflective
A network of rivers
　　　Water, connective
Your boat drifting downstream
　　　Water, directive
A storm in the city
　　　Water, objective
One drop on your eyelash
　　　Water, selective

Meandering

Something in water loves

                        the curve

        the bend

                    the zigzag

        the swerve.

Water will never be the type

        to prefer the ditch

the canal

                the pipe.

Rain running down

        a windowpane

                    or river rushing

through a state,

        water chooses

                            crooked.

It doesn't care for

        straight.

Something in water finds it grander

        to be commander

                        of meander.

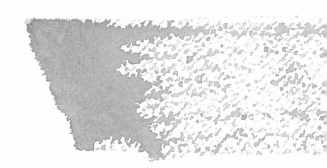

39

Ocean Checklist

Vast, blue-green or winter gray.

Tastes like salt, sends up spray.

Feeds its fishes, also whales.

Knows of breezes, also gales.

Changes tides and rolls out waves.

Sometimes sings and sometimes raves.

Welcomes ships at work or leisure—

Swallows some and hoards their treasure.

Likes to give and likes to keep.

Is everybody's dream of deep.

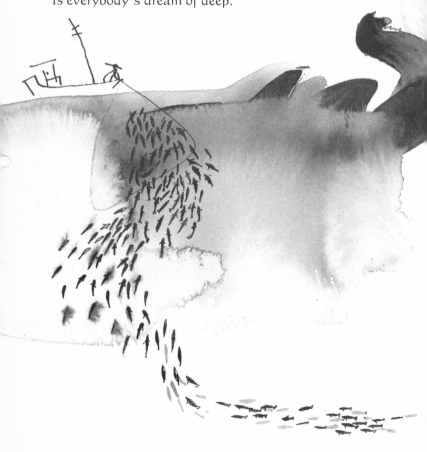